Jesus,
God's gift at
Christmas

Adrian Plass

Published by Verité CM Ltd. 2010

ISBN No. 978-1-907636-12-7

Cover image © Christian Publishing and Outreach Ltd.

All design, print and production management by
Verité CM Ltd, Worthing, West Sussex BN12 4HJ. UK.
www.veritecm.com

Printed in England

1.
THE CURSE
OF THE UNWANTED GIFT

We were given a picture for Christmas once. It was horrible. When exposed to view in any room (however small) it made the whole house seem like one of those dank, dark places where things die miserably because they haven't been properly fed or watered. Ironically, it was our dear friend Maisie who afflicted us with this monstrosity (her sad decease a couple of years ago allows me to tell the story at last), and she presented it one morning in December with coy pride.

"I dunno nuffink about pictures an' that," she said, her cheeks flushed cherry-red with the sheer pleasure of giving, "but I remember you an' Bridget sayin' you reely like modern art, so…" triumphantly – "I've got you some!"

Obscurely unnerved by the notion of acquiring 'some modern art' as you might acquire quantities of bacon and milk by the pound or the gallon, Bridget and I flicked a sideways glance at each other with a wild and fearful surmise, then set about removing a huge, hellishly pink bow and several layers of wrapping from the picture-shaped object that Maisie had dragged into the hall. As we unstuck bits of sellotape and pulled sheets of bubble-wrap apart we emitted little bleats of bright, excited anticipation. We were very fond of brittle, battered little Maisie, tottering around the world on her ridiculously high heels. This gift was going to be appreciated, even if it killed us.

And it nearly did. Fortunately, our response was blessedly ambiguous. Jaw-dropping, pop-eyed amazement might just as easily indicate wild delight as profound disgust, don't you think?

Oh, dear, how can I begin to convey the awfulness of that picture? Try to Imagine one of those semi-transparent, bottom-feeding horrors that crawl across the floor of the Marianas Trench, being melted with a blowtorch, encased in a pile of lime-green jelly and plonked on top of a virulently orange-coloured, flattened snowball. Do you have that image in your head? It was like that but much worse.

A label attached to the bottom of the ridiculously ornate, gold-painted plastic frame informed us that our new picture was entitled:

YES
– BUT NOT YET

Bridget recovered first, as usual.

"That is something, Maisie! Adrian, look, isn't that something?"

I agreed enthusiastically that it was something. Well, it was something. No word of a lie. It definitely was something.

Half an hour later the framed luminous pustule was hanging on the wall above the mantelpiece in our lounge. Any sense of hope or optimism had already drained from the room. A residual sludge of dull despair remained. The three of us stood and stared at the picture. Maisie's seedily pretty, good-natured face was alight with the satisfied but modest expression common to all generous benefactors. Bridget and I had both opted for a small contented smile and a slow, significant nodding movement of the head. 'At last,' our smiles and nods were intended to communicate, 'this room is truly complete'.

I leaned across until my mouth was close to Bridget's ear and whispered, "We are going to take the damn thing down, aren't we?"

Her reply, delivered out of the side of her mouth sounded like the worst excesses of bad ventriloquism and was almost inaudible.

"Yes, but not yet…"

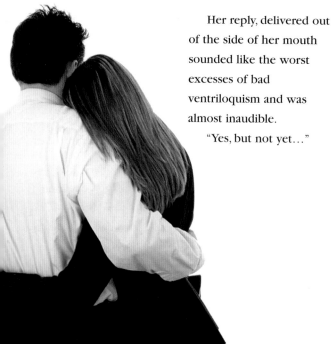

We did, of course, remove and replace the hideous object as soon as our visitor was off the premises, but this act of benevolent deceit spawned a succession of small nightmares. Maisie's treks across town to visit our home were never planned in advance, so her arrival at the front door invariably precipitated a minor panic, not least because her first question, delivered on the doorstep with a charmingly proprietary air, was likely to be, "How's the picture?" She seemed to think it might have developed a bit of a chill, or a slight backache.

The routine on these occasions was always the same for Bridget and me. After flashing urgent eye signals to each other, one of us would steer her forcibly through to the kitchen to be shown some very unremarkable spoon or bowl or utensil (Maisie was very open to being amazed and impressed by just about anything), while the other one dragged the picture out of the cupboard under the stairs, gave it a perfunctory dust, and exchanged it for the exquisite pencil drawing of Jaqueline Du Pré that normally graced the space over our mantelpiece. When only one of us was at home it became a rather more major panic, but we always managed it by hook or by crook.

It was tiring, though, and there were times when we wondered if a much larger lie would have been preferable. Might we have claimed, for instance, that because we believed such a valuable and important work should be available to the nation, we had sent it to the Tate Gallery, an institution that would have been beyond the outermost edges of Maisie's comprehension? Or, a much more radical alternative, would it have been better to simply tell the truth? Surely not…

2

WHY IT MIGHT BE
A SERIOUSLY BAD IDEA
TO FOLLOW JESUS

Now, you must be nervously anticipating, having glanced at the title of this booklet and the illustration on its cover, that this might well be the point where the gentle storytelling ends and the hard Christian sell begins. Something along the following lines, perhaps:

'When we unwrapped Maisie's present we discovered a gift that we really didn't want. When you decide to unwrap God's free gift of Jesus, however, you will discover something – or rather someone – who will satisfy your deepest needs, lasting you for the rest of your life and on into eternity. Just open the box and receive him into your life…'

No, I don't think so. I don't think I shall go there. You see, I wanted to tell the Maisie story as an indication to you the reader, and a reminder to myself, that telling the truth right at the beginning can save an awful lot of trouble later on. I fear that in the rather frantically positive world of evangelical Christianity (a world that I am part of in an angst-ridden sort of way) the truth of what it means to follow Jesus can be obscured by a passionate but unconsidered desire to superficially increase the size of the club at any cost. I understand that driving motivation, but unless the whole thing is explained properly it doesn't help. It really doesn't. I meet and hear from many, many folk who signed up, as it were, for a promising excursion that ultimately failed to reach its advertised destination, leaving them stranded in a small, sad little siding. You might be one of them.

There is one problem shared by almost all of these disappointed travellers. They have, if you will excuse the abrupt change of metaphor, thrown the baby out with the bathwater, but retained a deep and unfulfilled yearning for the infant hope that was beginning to grow in them. What is that hope, and how can it be retrieved and nurtured? We'll come back to that a little later.

In the meantime, what is this 'truth' that needs to be told?

Well, first I have to tell you that even if you did decide it was a good thing to become a follower of Jesus, he might not agree with you. It has always seemed strange to me that so much modern evangelism invites people to commitment with such seductively gentle phrases as *'Just come, just come…'*.

This kind of invitation has a slightly romantic, softly billowing silky feel about it, but Jesus was a carpenter and an essentially practical man, particularly in such down to earth matters as spirituality. He was at pains to explain to would-be disciples how important it was to know what would be expected of them in the long term. In the same way that a builder has to sit down and plan the cost of a project, he said, so anyone who genuinely wishes to follow him must do the same.

What is he talking about? What is the cost?
A couple of things spring immediately to mind.
One is about identity.

A young man came to see Jesus once. He seems to
have been a fine young fellow, morally upright and
seriously keen to know if it was possible to live forever,
and how one might go about doing it. Jesus really liked
the look of him.

"There's only one thing you're lacking," he said.
"Sell everything you've got, give the money away to
the poor and come along with me."

He couldn't do it.
This charming, extremely
rich young man couldn't
do it. And it probably wasn't
about the money itself.
It was about giving away
the aspect of his life that
made him what he was in
his own eyes, his identity.

Naked and embarrassed without the cash. That was the picture he couldn't handle. He was terribly sad as he went away. Jesus didn't try to stop him as far as we know. The cost had been too much. I do hope he sorted it later.

So how about that, then? It's a heavy call. Money, fame, gardening, women, men, pacifism, aggression, all sorts of fine and admirable principles, it could be anything. You may or may not be actually asked to give it all away, but you can't depend on it, and you can't allow it to define the person that you are. Finding out your identity in Jesus is all He is interested in. Scary, eh?

What else? Safety. Do you want to give that up? I'm talking about safety as most of the world would understand it. Jesus clearly has no intention of offering that kind of security. Call it divine madness or call it adventure, call it whatever you like, but be aware that if you go with him, although the central, most important part of you will never be dented, let alone destroyed, anything could happen to the frail shell we call the body. There is no guaranteed protection of that sort. Sometimes the storms will rage and there will be no shore in sight. You will be very afraid, and very glad that you know someone who seems able to walk on water and, amazingly, get tough with the weather.

Worth the risk? I suppose that is the question we all have to ask and answer at some point in our lives.

I have only described two areas of cost. There are others. Personal agenda, cherished certainties, choice in all sorts of situations, self-reliance. All of these things have to be held so lightly that they can be dropped at a moment's notice.

But enough of all that. It is too depressing for words. As time goes by the cost will be revealed as total and uncompromising. Why would anyone want to pay it? When we unwrap this gift of Jesus, what exactly will we be getting? It had better be worth it.

3
PARCELS IN THE PILLOWCASE

When we were young, my brothers and I didn't have stockings at Christmas. We had pillowcases. Much better, of course, because they were bigger and could hold more presents. Nothing will ever quite compare with the excitement of reaching out in the dark at some unearthly hour of the morning to run my hand around the edges of those packages, trying to work out from the shapes what they might contain. The gift of Jesus comes in a variety of parcels. Let's look at some of them. They may help us to understand the nature of those babies I mentioned earlier, the ones that have been slung out with the bathwater, and need to be recovered and looked after with fierce determination and tender care.

The first package feels like a book. Correct.

It is a book, one made up of lots of other books, filled with history and poetry and stories and teaching and the anatomy of a mystery that inhabits the heart of everything that ever was or is or will be. Long, long ago something went dreadfully, drastically wrong with this world. The gap that developed between God and human beings as a result could only be closed by Jesus, who, through an inexplicable process of terrible death and miraculous recovery healed the wound of separation and made it possible for all of us, God as well, to inherit the best of all possible worlds. This book has generated conflict, resolution, peace, debate, healing and inspiration for centuries. So it should. The heart of the mystery and its solution is here.

The next gift is simply an envelope, but it is a golden envelope. Inside there is an extract from the book, a written promise that, if you wish, you can be wealthy beyond your wildest dreams. Forget winning the lottery. Ten million pounds is peanuts compared with this. We can be fabulously rich, suggested Jesus. We can store up treasure in heaven through co-operation and identification with his work in this world, and enjoy spending it when we eventually join him.

Be careful. Some people claim that when Jesus said things like this he was speaking in pictures that have no substance. Of course, they say, there is no real treasure in heaven. Nor are there mansions specially prepared for us to live in. We shall not actually be reunited with those we love in any meaningful way. The new heaven and the new earth are simply metaphors.

That's OK, people can believe all those things if they wish. We shall see. Some of us might be very surprised.

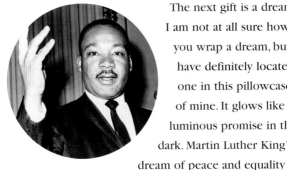

The next gift is a dream. I am not at all sure how you wrap a dream, but I have definitely located one in this pillowcase of mine. It glows like a luminous promise in the dark. Martin Luther King's dream of peace and equality was an inspired image of the future, but even that extraordinary vision was only a tiny part of the big picture that is presented to us.

This dream is made possible through that mysterious process by which Jesus died and came back to life and thereby overcame the dismal inevitability of death and disappointment. At that moment the ancient, massive engines of fundamental order and rightness were fuelled and fired up and set in motion for the first time since men and women lost the right to walk easily and happily with God in the cool of the afternoon.

It is a dream of loose ends tied up, the reuniting of those who have loved and lost each other, the repair of broken hearts and wasted lives, the establishment of justice with mercy, a discovery of peace in people and situations that seemed beyond hope. This dream allows a breathlessly beautiful re-acquaintance with our lost innocence, a robustly childlike confidence in a truth expressed by the mystic Julian of Norwich when she wrote that: 'all shall be well, and all shall be well, and all manner of things shall be well'.

Just enough space to mention one more gift, strangely shaped this one, and not easy to explain. It is the gift of a person and a power. The book describes how Jesus came across a woman who was taking the body of her son to be interred. Not surprisingly she was weeping. His heart went out to her.

'Don't cry,' said Jesus.

Very poor counselling technique, as anyone involved in that fine profession will tell you. Urging sufferers to dab their eyes and pull themselves together is very rarely profitable – unless, that is, you are able to remove the reason for their pain. Jesus prayed for the young man and he came back to life. Compassion coupled with power is a mindboggling combination.

God is commonly spoken of as being three persons in one. Not three functions, like the old vacuum cleaners that were supposed to 'beat as they sweep as they clean', but three distinct people who, nevertheless, are one. (By the way, if you think I understand what I've written with such confidence, you are sadly mistaken. I just know the theory.) One of these is God the Father, one is Jesus, the Son, and one is the Holy Spirit. It is the gift of this third person and his power to change things in the world, that I am struggling to explain.

After coming back from the dead Jesus told his disciples that it was necessary for him to return to his Father so that the Holy Spirit could come and live in the lives of men and women who have decided to follow Jesus. He would be the compassion and power of God in the hearts of these followers, guiding and inspiring and even, from time to time, providing words when they are most needed and the human mind is at its most gormlessly blank.

OK, let me be honest, the spiritual plumbing and mechanics involved in all this are completely beyond me, but I can say that it seems to have worked. Leaving aside the idiotic nonsenses and distortions with which we Christians continually shoot ourselves in both mouth-occupying feet (someone should definitely illustrate that), there is impressive evidence that the Holy Spirit does actually work with power, particularly when his 'vessels' manage to curb their religious mania, get out of the way and remain content to be vessels.

There we are then. Wonderful gifts, and if I had more time and space I could tell you of others.

4

SO WHAT?

Yes, so what? The cost of this 'gift' is total, the rewards are immense, and, just to make the whole thing more complicated, the business of 'living the Christian life', whatever that means, is very far from easy. I am a follower of Jesus, and I have known ecstasy, despair, total doubt, absolute faith, amazement at the things God does through his followers, and a combination of fury and disappointment when he doesn't do the things that seem blindingly obvious and necessary to my huge brain. What a rich mixture of experiences I have known over more than four decades of wrestling with it all. Have I learned anything?

First, I am aware that there is much more going on behind the scenes than I realised. A vast amount of urgent, passionately fuelled organisation is happening in some invisible spiritual realm, so that quite ordinary events can happen appropriately and usefully in this world. I think we would be amazed.

Second, I realise now that I know next to nothing about anything. As I have certainly said before, I am like a child walking through a shopping mall with his dad. I don't know where we're going or what's going to happen when we get there. I just hold my Father's hand and do my best to trust him. He must know what he's doing, surely?

Third, and perhaps most important, despite and because of everything, I love Jesus. I don't care what anyone thinks about that. I can't help it. I just do. He's been a nightlight in the darkness and a beacon on a hill and a silver lining on the edge of some terrifyingly black clouds for as long as I can remember.

And, in the end, I think that this creative relationship with Jesus is the 'baby' lost by those people I mentioned earlier. They got bullied or hurt or confused and they threw the whole thing away, only to discover that something true and beautiful got dumped and lost in the process. To them I would like to say, 'You are allowed to have your baby back. Look after it this time. Don't let anyone take it away again. It's yours.'

And what can I say to those who have never unwrapped the gift of Jesus? I hope you count the cost. Take your time. But I also hope, from the bottom of my heart, that you will do what the prodigal did in the story that Jesus told. You can read about it in the second section of the book, in the fifteenth chapter of Luke.

I hope that you will decide to turn your back on whatever needs to be left behind in your life, and go home to the place you have missed for years without ever knowing what or where it is.

You will be warmly welcomed by the Father, and there will be a party, and your life will change.

You will still have lots of problems, but they will be so much easier to tackle when you are a son or daughter in that household.

And all this will be made possible by Jesus, who is regarding you with a quizzical look at this very moment. One day we shall fully understand at last what he did to get us home. He gave himself for us. What a gift.